My First French
Alphabets

Picture Book with English Translations

Published By: MyFirstPictureBook.com

Aa

L'arbre

Tree

Bb

Le bateau

Boat

Cc

La chaise

Chair

Dd

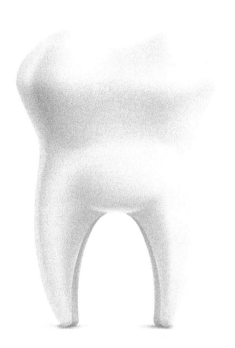

La dent

Tooth

Ee

L'eau

Water

Ff

La fleur

Flower

Gg

La glace

Ice

Hh

L'horloge

Clock

Ii

L'île

Island

Jj

Le jardin

Garden

Kk

Le kangourou

Kangaroo

Ll

Le lait

Milk

Mm

La maison

House

Nn

Le nuage

Cloud

Oo

L'oiseau

Bird

Pp

Le pain

Bread

Qq

Le coq

Rooster (Male Chicken)

Rr

La roue

Wheel

Ss

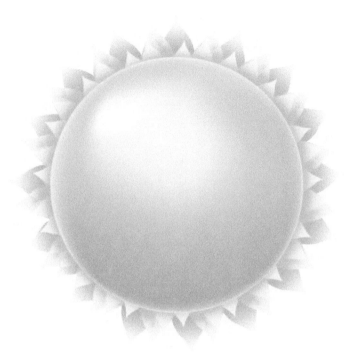

Le soleil

Sun

Tt

Le tapis

Carpet

Uu

Le gâteau

Cake

Vv

La valise

Suitcase

Ww

Le site web

Website

Xx

La noix

Walnut

Yy

Le yaourt

Yogurt

Zz

Le riz

Rice

CPSIA information can be obtained
at www.ICGtesting.com
Printed in the USA
LVHW070951181121
703711LV00023B/400